Are social networking sites
harmful?

⌐ DUE

At Issue

Are Social Networking Sites Harmful?

Other Books in the At Issue Series:

At Issue

Are Social Networking Sites Harmful?

Stefan Kiesbye, Book Editor

GREENHAVEN PRESS
A part of Gale, Cengage Learning

GALE
CENGAGE Learning™

Detroit • New York • San Francisco • New Haven, Conn • Waterville, Maine • London

2/11   # 6425 10188

Christine Nasso, *Publisher*
Elizabeth Des Chenes, *Managing Editor*

For more information, contact:
Greenhaven Press
27500 Drake Rd.
Farmington Hills, MI 48331-3535
Or you can visit our Internet site at gale.cengage.com

For product information and technology assistance, contact us at

Gale Customer Support, 1-800-877-4253
For permission to use material from this text or product, submit all requests online at
www.cengage.com/permissions

Further permissions questions can be e-mailed to permissionrequest@cengage.com

Articles in Greenhaven Press anthologies are often edited for length to meet page requirements. In addition, original titles of these works are changed to clearly present the main thesis and to explicitly indicate the author's opinion. Every effort is made to ensure that Greenhaven Press accurately reflects the original intent of the authors. Every effort has been made to trace the owners of copyrighted material.

LIBRARY OF CONGRESS CATALOGING-IN-PUBLICATION DATA

Are social networking sites harmful? / Stefan Kiesbye, book editor.
    p. cm. -- (At issue)
Includes bibliographical references and index.
ISBN 978-0-7377-5131-4 (hardcover) -- ISBN 978-0-7377-5132-1 (pbk.)
1. Online social networks--Juvenile literature. 2. Internet and children--Juvenile literature. 3. Internet and teenagers--Juvenile literature. 4. Internet--Safety measures. I. Kiesbye, Stefan.
    HM742.A74 2010
    302.30285--dc22

                                                    2010024368

Printed in the United States of America
1 2 3 4 5 6 7 14 13 12 11 10

Contents

Introduction

Social networking sites have sparked a revolution of how people connect to friends, family, and "friends"—relative strangers, friends of a friend, or people with shared interests suggested by the site itself. Status updates keep users informed about what everyone in their network is doing, pictures can be uploaded and shared, and invitations to events can be extended. In addition, sites like Facebook allow a user to shape an online identity; on Facebook everyone can be what they aspire to be. As with any new technology or pop culture phenomenon, however, some commentators have expressed concern about the safety of these sites.

Media critics and others have voiced unease about various aspects of social networking sites. Some fear that sexual predators will befriend unsuspecting teenagers via Facebook or MySpace. Others point to the possibility of identity theft and believe that social networking sites might erode real-life friendships or cause obesity. The news media has often increased these fears, highlighting disturbing, mostly isolated, episodes involving MySpace and Facebook.

When suburban mother Lori Drew created a fake account on MySpace—impersonating a male teenager—and began a relationship with Megan Meier, a teen and former friend of her daughter, many blamed her for Meier's eventual suicide. The case against Drew—she was acquitted on all four counts of the indictment, ranging from computer fraud to conspiracy—became famous. This was the first widely discussed case of cyberbullying involving social networking sites, but other crimes have followed.

On January 23, 2009, the news site Breitbart.com reported on the case of Edward Richardson, a forty-one-year-old man, who killed his estranged wife Sarah, twenty-six, because she had changed her Facebook relationship status from married to single. "[Richardson] gained entry by breaking the front door window and made his way into the property. Once inside, he found Sarah in her bedroom and subjected her to a frenzied and brutal attack with a knife and then attempted to take his own life."

On February 9, 2009, James Tazor of the British *Daily Mail* reported the "world's first divorce by Facebook." Emma Brady, a thirty-five-year-old event organizer, received word that her husband, Neil, had posted a message on Facebook. "It read: 'Neil Brady has ended his marriage to Emma Brady.'" The wife was blindsided by the announcement, and when she later confronted her husband, "he acted like everything was fine so we carried on as normal." Several months later, Neil Brady was convicted of assaulting his wife during a fight.

To a casual observer, evidence seems to be mounting that Facebook and other social networking sites are to blame for bullying and violence, but the issue is far more complex than what the cited cases and many others like them suggest. Cases such as those involving Lori Drew, the Richardsons, and the Bradys often involve contact and circumstances offline that are not captured in the headlines, which frequently serve to raise concerns among parents and others. Indeed the influence and power of Facebook and other social networking sites might be overestimated by critics.

According to the September 14, 2007, issue of *Science Daily*, researcher Will Reader of Sheffield Hallam University found that "some 90 per cent of the online friends rated as 'close' have been met face-to-face, with the remaining 10 per cent likely to be friends of close friends. . . ." Young people might connect more easily to others via social networking sites, but they still don't stray far. Facebook and MySpace seem to be used most often as extensions of real-world friendships, not as replacements.

Daniel S. Halder, of the University of Chicago, goes even further. In the paper "Ethnographic Study of the Effects of

Facebook.com on Interpersonal Relationships," published on April 16, 2006, he suggests that the social networking site does not "prevent or hinder other forms of interaction." The time spent of Facebook does not seem to cut into face-to-face time. In fact, he concludes that "Facebook.com does not create or spur new social relationships or . . . even interfere with existing ones, but . . . it only augments existing ties."

The debate about whether social networking sites are harmful will continue to be played out in the media and among commentators. The authors of the following viewpoints offer their opinions on whether social networking sites have proved to be harmful to users. Their voices add to this contentious but necessary debate.

Social Networking Sites Help Students Gain Important Skills

Lauren Gerber

Lauren Gerber writes on computer and technology issues for PC1News.com.

Far from being a source of distraction and danger, social networking sites offer teenagers the opportunity to navigate everyday technology, learn valuable computer and social skills, and polish their language proficiency. Acquiring computer skills will help them find jobs later in their careers and prepares them for a professional environment in which computers are commonplace.

In the world that we live in, the majority of people can't survive without the internet. People tend to use a computer or the internet at least once a day to achieve at least one thing. Children of all ages usually have better internet skills than their parents. Teenagers are learning how to hack and can gain access into huge computer systems from very early ages. It is not uncommon today to associate jobs in computers with a wonderful modern lifestyle filled with the best material luxuries that money can buy. There is money in computers and some people who work in the I.T. industry will be set financially for the rest of their lives. Latest surveys have discovered that there are actually lots of benefits for teenagers who are online a lot.

The Benefits of Online Networking

We all hear so many stories with regard to the dangers of the internet for teenagers. The good news is that teenagers are actually gaining many benefits by going online a lot. If your teenage son or daughter is spending more time on a social networking site or a blog than doing homework then this may actually not be a bad thing. For starters your teenager is acquiring new computer skills every day. The thing that parents don't know is that even simply going on Facebook is teaching your teenager how to use the internet to their advantage. The majority of sites that are popular amongst teenagers are actually sites which require some degree of computer skills. The more computer skills that your teenager gains the more chances there are of your teenager landing a job within a huge computer company.

The skills that your teenager is acquiring by spending so much time online will prove very useful for their future. Even if your teenager does not want to work in a big computer company one day, computers are being used for everything. You can never go wrong with computer skills and the more skills that you have with computers the more chances that you have in the world. There are so many computer related jobs out there that spending lots of time online is actually a good thing.

The thing that parents don't know is that even simply going on Facebook is teaching your teenager how to use the internet to their advantage.

Learning New Skills

Each moment that your teenager is spending online they are learning new things. Teenagers are learning how to get along with other people through socializing on various online sites. Being able to communicate with people and respect their differences as individuals is a skill that will prove extremely helpful in their future. Your teenager may actually be learning how to create a web site, how to advertise effectively or even how to program. Without you realizing it, all the time that your teenager is spending online which you may be complaining about, may actually be teaching them lots of different skills which they may need for their future.

The internet is also helping your teenager's English ability. By constantly reading and being exposed to words and spelling your teenagers English is actually improving. Anything that your teenager reads online is actually improving their literacy skills. By constantly being online teenagers are teaching themselves how to navigate their way around the internet as well as how to use the search engines. The amount of skills that your teenagers are learning just by being online will be extremely beneficial for their future. The next time that you get irritated because you teenager is spending too much time online just stop to consider all the skills they are gaining from being online.

Social Networking Sites Can Limit Interpersonal Skills and Physical Activity

Sue Scheff

Sue Scheff is a parent advocate and founder of the organization Parent's Universal Resource Experts, which supports and educates parents of troubled teens. She is also the author of Wit's End: Advice and Resources for Saving Your Out-of-Control Teen.

While the Internet is a helpful and accurate source of knowledge and an easy-to-use means of worldwide communications, its social networking features can lead to addiction in teenagers. In extreme cases, it can limit young adults' personal growth and thwart social development. Furthermore, the Internet makes it easy for sexual predators to contact their prey and harm teenagers, who are seduced by sexually explicit content. Finally, Internet addiction might cause teenagers to neglect physical activity and lead a secluded, unhealthy life.

In today's society, the Internet has made its way into almost every American home. It is a well-known fact that the web is a valuable asset for research and learning. Unfortunately, it can also be a very dangerous place for teens. With social networking sites like Myspace and Friendster, chat rooms, instant messaging, and online role-playing video games, our children are at access to almost anyone. Sue Scheff, along with Parent's Universal Resource Experts™, is tackling the dangers of the web.

Sue Scheff, "Wrapped Up In the Web: The Dangers of Teen Internet Addiction," www.sue-scheff.net, 2007. Reproduced by permission of the author.

Keeping tabs on our teens' online habits doesn't just keep them safe from online predators. More and more parents are becoming wary of the excessive hours their teens spend surfing the web, withdrawing from family, friends and activities they used to enjoy. Internet Addiction is a devastating problem facing far too many teens and their families. While medical professionals have done limited research on the topic, more and more are recognizing this destructive behavior and even more, the potential mental effects it can have.

Though the web is a great place for learning and can be safe for keeping in touch, it is important that families understand the potential risks and dangers to find a healthy balance between real and virtual life.

The Dangers of Teen Internet Addiction

It's clear that, for teenagers, spending too much time online can really deter social and educational development. The Internet world is such that there is always something new to do and to distract one from one's responsibilities. We all do it—take ten minutes here or there to explore our favorite gossip or sports site. There is nothing wrong with using the Internet as a tool for research, news, and even entertainment. After all, the World Wide Web is the world's most accurate, up to date resource for almost any type of information.

But as the Internet evolves and becomes more tailored to the individual, it grows increasingly easier to develop a dependency on it. This is especially true for teens—a group that tends to be susceptible to flashy graphics and easily enticed by the popularity of social networks. In a sense, the Internet is the new video game or TV show. It used to be that adolescents would sit in front of the TV for hours on end operating a remote, shooting people and racing cars. Now they surf the web. Teens are impressionable and can at times be improperly equipped to handle certain situations with a degree of reason and rationality. And although they may have good intentions, they might be at risk of coming across something inappropriate and even dangerous.

Sexual Predators

We've all heard the stories about children entering chat rooms who end up talking to someone older than them who may be looking for something more than merely a chat. These tales may sound far-fetched, or to some, even mundane, because of the publicity they've received, but as a parent it would be rather foolish to dismiss them as hearsay or as something that could never actually happen to your child. The fact is, these accounts of sexual predation are all too true and have caused some families a great deal of strain and fear. Even pre-adolescents have been known to join chat rooms. The reality is that there is no real way of knowing who might be in one at any given time. An even scarier thought is that these forums are often sexual predators' main source of contact with young children. In fact, the popular TV show, *To Catch a Predator* . . . employs someone to pose as a teen and entice these sex offenders. The show profiles the interactions between them all the way up until the actual meeting. Some of the situations portrayed are horrifying. . . .

[A]s the Internet evolves and becomes more tailored to the individual, it grows increasingly easier to develop a dependency on it.

Sensitive Subject Matter

Human curiosity is perhaps at its peak during one's teenage years. That curiosity is what aids teens in the growth and development process. It's necessary for survival as an adolescent and can provide for some great discoveries and maturation. However, teen curiosity can also potentially lead a person into some questionable situations, and the Internet is a prime medium through which to quell one's inquisitiveness. Let's face it—teenagers are anxious to be knowledgeable about topics such as sex, drugs, and other dangerous subject matter. . . .

The Internet might be an excellent tool for presenting interesting data, but it can also grossly misrepresent certain issues. If a teenager wants to learn about sex or drugs via the web, he or she might decide to do a search containing the words "sex" or, perhaps "marijuana." The results your child might find may not necessarily be the type of educational, instructive material you'd hope they would receive. The Internet may be savvy, but one thing it's not capable of doing is knowing who is using it at any given time and how to customize its settings. . . .

Limited Social Growth

There is no better time to experience new things and meet new people than during one's teenage years. Getting outside, going to social gatherings, and just having a good time with friends are among some of the most productive and satisfying activities in which teenagers can engage. While the Internet can provide a degree of social interaction, online networks and connections cannot replace the benefits of in-person contact. Teen Internet Addiction is dangerous because it limits a person's options when it comes to communication. Much of learning and growing as a teen comes from the lessons one learns through friendships, fights, disagreements, trends, popularity, etc.

The Internet has made it all too easy for teens to recoil from the pressures of adolescence and remain indoors. The lure of the web can often make it seem as though social networks and online gaming are acceptable substitutes for real life. Teens can find acceptance in chat rooms and message boards, while at school they might be complete outcasts. It's easy for teenagers to rebuff the idea of interacting with their peers and risking rejection when the Internet can provide for a seemingly relaxed environment. Children need to know that Internet addiction and reliance on online forums will only stunt social growth and make life much more difficult in the future.

The Internet might be an excellent tool for presenting interesting data, but it can also grossly misrepresent certain issues.

Sedentary Lifestyle

Internet dependency also inherently promotes a lifestyle that is not conducive to exercise and physical activity. Many teens tend to become so enthralled in games or chats that peeling them away from the computer can prove to be an ominous task. The entertainment the Internet can provide often trumps the option to leave the house and get exercise. Parents should encourage their teens to use the Internet for school projects and some degree of entertainment, but they should also limit the time that they are allowed to spend on the computer. . . . The earlier a child is introduced to the mental and physical benefits of outside activity, the more likely he or she is to avoid inside amusements such as the Internet, TV, and video games.

Nowadays it seems our whole lives can be conducted via the Internet. We can order, purchase, and have groceries delivered all with the click of a few buttons. We can play games, talk to people, find dates, and even attend AA meetings online. The Internet may have made our lives and their day-to-day processes exponentially easier to accomplish, but by the same token it has also increased our dependence on the advantages it can provide. The convenience it creates has been known to cause some people to recoil from outside situations, opting to conduct as much business as possible from home.

We must be careful of this trend, especially with teenagers, for whom positive (and negative) social interaction help to form valuable personality and wisdom.

3

Social Networking Sites Harm Children's Brains

David Derbyshire

David Derbyshire is the Daily Mail's *environment editor. He has worked as a journalist for various British newspapers since 1996.*

Social networking sites shorten teenagers' attention span, and lead to egotistical and antisocial behaviors. The more time children spend in front of the computer, the more their natural brain development is damaged. Their brains are rewired, causing them to look for instant gratification and leading them away from healthy real-life social interactions.

Social networking websites are causing alarming changes in the brains of young users, an eminent scientist has warned.

Sites such as Facebook, Twitter and Bebo are said to shorten attention spans, encourage instant gratification and make young people more self-centered.

The claims from neuroscientist Susan Greenfield will make disturbing reading for the millions whose social lives depend on logging on to their favourite websites each day.

But they will strike a chord with parents and teachers who complain that many youngsters lack the ability to communicate or concentrate away from their screens.

More than 150 million use Facebook to keep in touch with friends, share photographs and videos and post regular updates of their movements and thoughts.

A further six million have signed up to Twitter, the 'micro-blogging' service that lets users circulate text messages about themselves.

Sites such as Facebook, Twitter and Bebo are said to shorten attention spans, encourage instant gratification and make young people more self-centred.

But while the sites are popular—and extremely profitable—a growing number of psychologists and neuroscientists believe they may be doing more harm than good.

Rewiring the Brain

Baroness Greenfield, an Oxford University neuroscientist and director of the Royal Institution, believes repeated exposure could effectively 'rewire' the brain.

Computer games and fast-paced TV shows were also a factor, she said.

'We know how small babies need constant reassurance that they exist,' she told the Mail yesterday.

'My fear is that these technologies are infantilising the brain into the state of small children who are attracted by buzzing noises and bright lights, who have a small attention span and who live for the moment.'

Her comments echoed those she made during a House of Lords debate earlier this month [February 2009]. Then she argued that exposure to computer games, instant messaging, chat rooms and social networking sites could leave a generation with poor attention spans.

'I often wonder whether real conversation in real time may eventually give way to these sanitised and easier screen dialogues, in much the same way as killing, skinning and butchering an animal to eat has been replaced by the convenience of packages of meat on the supermarket shelf,' she said.

Lady Greenfield told the Lords a teacher of 30 years had told her she had noticed a sharp decline in the ability of her pupils to understand others.

'It is hard to see how living this way on a daily basis will not result in brains, or rather minds, different from those of previous generations,' she said.

She pointed out that autistic people, who usually find it hard to communicate, were particularly comfortable using computers.

'Of course, we do not know whether the current increase in autism is due more to increased awareness and diagnosis of autism or whether it can—if there is a true increase—be in any way linked to an increased prevalence among people of spending time in screen relationships. Surely it is a point worth considering,' she added.

Most games only trigger the 'flight or fight' region of the brain, rather than the vital areas responsible for reasoning.

Changing the Mind

Psychologists have also argued that digital technology is changing the way we think. They point out that students no longer need to plan essays before starting to write—thanks to word processors they can edit as they go along. Satellite navigation systems have negated the need to decipher maps.

A study by the Broadcaster Audience Research Board found teenagers now spend seven-and-a-half hours a day in front of a screen.

Educational psychologist Jane Healy believes children should be kept away from computer games until they are seven.

Most games only trigger the 'flight or fight' region of the brain, rather than the vital areas responsible for reasoning.

Sue Palmer, author of Toxic Childhood, said: 'We are seeing children's brain development damaged because they don't engage in the activity they have engaged in for millennia.

'I'm not against technology and computers. But before they start social networking, they need to learn to make real relationships with people.'

4

Social Networking Sites Can Be Forums for Cyberbullying

Abraham Foxman and Cyndi Silverman

Abraham Foxman is the national director of the Anti-Defamation League and the author of the book Never Again? The Threat of the New Anti-Semitism. *Cyndi Silverman is director of the Anti-Defamation League's Santa Barbara regional office.*

While hate and prejudice are as old as humankind, new technologies have helped to spread them quicker and more forcefully than ever before. The Internet has created racist forums and communities, and new social networking sites draw in teenagers and enable them to spread vicious rumors about classmates and neighbors. Cyberbullying has become a real threat, and parents and educators must work in unison to counter antisocial and harmful harassment and make such crimes punishable by law.

Hate has always been with us. Racism, anti-Semitism, and other forms of prejudice have always infected society at some level.

Historically it has come in many forms—in leaflets handed out from a paper bag on a street corner, in racist rallies and speeches and, occasionally, even from the pulpit. But in today's world there is a new, more insidious and effective delivery system for the age-old virus of hate. In many ways it is more potent, more virulent, and more threatening than anything we have seen in the past. It is, simply put, the ability to spread words of hate electronically.

Abraham Foxman and Cyndi Silverman, "Op Ed," *Anti-Defamation League*, December 7, 2009. Reproduced by permission.

Spreading Hate Online

It started with the Internet. While this technology held out the promise of a new era for interconnectedness, information-sharing and education, it also came with a dark underbelly, as bigots and anti-Semites found it a useful tool for propagating hatred. The Web sites they created have evolved over time and with the technology, yet they continue to be a very effective tool for spreading hatred, giving the bigots the ability to reach a potential audience of millions. Now, this ability to spread hateful sentiments electronically has reached new dimensions. It has taken on new life in the form of cyberbullying, or the ability to use (and abuse) the fairly new technologies of instant messaging, cell phones, texting, and online social-networking to harass and intimidate.

Nowhere has this new form of bullying been more prevalent than in middle and high schools. After all, it is teenage students who are most facile with these new technologies and who are most likely to employ them in a group social setting, such as school or camp. Indeed, the Internet, cell phones and other technological paraphernalia play a central role in the social lives of nearly all adolescents. While much of their online activity may be harmless enough, it has also provided an opening for would-be schoolyard bullies to spread innuendo, falsehoods and slander to dozens, even hundreds, of classmates with the touch of a button or click of a mouse. The real-world consequences of cyberbullying have been widely reported. We are familiar with the stories about children and teenagers driven to desperate, even suicidal acts after having been exposed to repeated harassment in cyberspace. We know that cyberbullying can damage reputations, and destroy lives. The level of hatred that can arise in a school setting, whether expressed in the virtual world or in the actual classroom or schoolyard, can be shocking even to those with dulled sensibilities.

Finding Ways to Curb Prejudice

The question for educators, parents and those of us who work every day to confront and counter prejudice in society is how to effectively address this new form of harassment. What tools do we have to fight back? How can we prevent students from using technology to do harm to others, and to ensure that students really understand the impact of hateful words?

There is no one panacea [a cure-all], of course. But there are those reliable and effective tools that we have traditionally had at our disposal to respond when prejudice rears its ugly head. They include, in no particular order: Education, awareness and advocacy. Education remains one of the most effective methods for fighting back against bigotry. For example, the Anti-Defamation League helps to put anti-bias training programs directly into the school setting with cyberbullying and anti-bias workshops for middle and high school educators and students. These trainings not only raise awareness of the dangers and effects of cyberbullying, but also provide practical information to help schools, teachers and administrators to develop comprehensive plans for prevention and for creating and maintaining a safe learning environment for students. Awareness helps students, teachers, parents and caregivers to identify prejudice or cyberbullying when it occurs.

We know that cyberbullying can damage reputations, and destroy lives.

Awareness enables people to speak out and to report expressions of hatred—both of the viral and face-to-face sorts—and to have a greater knowledge of the risk factor involved if people remain silent and allow acts of hatred to go left unchecked.

Lawmakers Need to Act

Finally, there is advocacy and—better yet—legislation. Over the past 10 years, 41 states, including California, have adopted laws mandating schools implement anti-bullying statutes. Some of these statutes offer general prohibitions against bullying, while others are more directed and specific. More states need to adopt comprehensive anti-bullying laws based on the ADL model, and some should revisit their statutes in light of the unique problem of cyberbullying in our increasingly wired-up and logged-in society. And for those states that do have comprehensive laws, like California, we should encourage and help schools to comply by creating and adhering to strong school policies.

We can rise above the statistics. We can keep our schools and communities safe from online and real-world hate. But first it takes a will and a determination to recognize the extent of the problem, to speak out and say "no" to prejudice and bigotry, and to take action. We must act now to ensure that those who would engage in harassment or bullying—whether on the street or in cyberspace—will face real-world consequences for their actions.

5

Social Networking Sites Cannot Be Blamed for Bullying

Kate Harding

Kate Harding is the coauthor of Lessons from the Fat-o-sphere: Quit Dieting and Declare a Truce with Your Body. *She is a blogger for* Shapely Prose *and a regular contributor to* Salon .com.

Despite nationwide outrage over cyberbullying, social networking sites such as Facebook and MySpace are not to blame for vile gossip or cafeteria brawls. Networking sites are only a new medium for teenagers to wage their wars—they don't create them. Educators and parents would be well advised not to demonize new computer technologies but instead to teach students responsible online behaviors. The Internet is here to stay, and draconian measures will only alienate teenagers instead of helping them to navigate social networking sites safely and without doing harm to others.

If you're a parent and/or educator of teenagers, you might want to sit down in your comfiest chair right now—perhaps with a nice, soothing cup of tea—because I'm about to drop some unfortunate news on you. Ready? Here it is: *The Internet is not going away anytime soon.*

What that means is, what appears to be an all-new host of teen problems—e.g., nasty rumors, numbskull comments and

Kate Harding, "More Teen Troubles Blamed on Social Networking," *Salon.com*, December 23, 2009. This article first appeared in Salon.com, at www.salon.com. An online version remains in the Salon archives. Reprinted with permission.

nudie pictures spreading not only throughout the school but *worldwide* in record time—will also be around for the foreseeable future. Which in turn means that railing about the dangers of Facebook and Twitter, and calling for kids to turn off their computers and get outside, is about as useful as decrying the pernicious [injurious or destructive] influence of Elvis's waggling hips.

A Fast-Changing World

You know that Beloit College "Mindset List" that comes around every fall, ostensibly to identify "the cultural touch-stones that shape the lives of students entering college" but actually just to make you feel f---ing ancient? Here are a few that pertain to the class of 2013: "Everyone has always known what the evening news was before the Evening News came on"; "migration of once independent media like radio, TV, videos and compact discs to the computer has never amazed them"; "they have always been able to read books on an electronic screen"; "text has always been hyper." It won't be too long before that list includes, "Social networking has existed for their entire lives." Adults may still see online communication as an optional complement (and potential detriment) to *real* interaction, but to the kids we're all so worried about, it's just as real as any other kind.

So, that's just one reason why I bristle (read: foam at the mouth) when I see educators (or parents or cops, whatever) saying things like, "Facebook was the only common denominator" with regard to bullying incidents. That particular quote came from David Heisey, principal of Scotch Plains-Fanwood High in New Jersey, about a cafeteria fight that apparently had its genesis on some kid's "wall." "The statements posted on Facebook led to statements that were exchanged in the cafeteria, which led to the girls fighting," says Heisey. And Facebook is the *only* common denominator he sees there? Really? One other that leaps out to me is: Scotch Plains-Fanwood High

School. Also, the cafeteria, the gender of the participants, and oh yes, the existence of some "statements" that set the whole thing off.

Cruelty Is Not Limited to Facebook

Which brings us to reason No. 2 why blaming Facebook for all manner of teen trouble drives me bats: It erases the underlying problem, which is *kids treating each other like crap*, not the specific vehicle for it. Norman Whitehouse, president of the Scotch Plains-Fanwood school board, offers a letter-perfect illustration of the curmudgeonly ostrich approach still favored by too many Concerned Adults: "This goes further than bullying 30 or 40 years ago, when you would get a bloody nose on the playground."

Just as Facebook is not causing the death of genuine friendship, it is also not causing the birth of high school enemies.

Let me just give you the bullet points of what's so painfully wrong with that line of thinking:

• Hey, guess what! It's not 30 or 40 years ago! It's right now!

• I don't know when it will hit the Beloit Mindset List, but we have known for some time that relational aggression A) exists, B) causes serious damage and C) has been practiced, especially by girls, for as long as anyone can remember. The idea that bullying always used to mean sucker-punching a boy for his lunch money, and therefore any other form of childhood aggression must be new and strange (and thus the direct result of new and strange things, like Facebook!) is both sexist and hopelessly outdated.

• Also sexist and outdated, not to mention ridiculous? The idea that getting "a bloody nose on the playground" was somehow *not* a real problem way back when, but today's kids are so much worse (and/or so much wimpier) than we were. Actually, they're pretty much doing what kids have always done to each other, just with more advanced technology. And getting sucker-punched, physically or emotionally, was always painful (even for boys!) no matter how tough you acted then or how much you've forgotten now.

Claiming that "Facebook is the only common denominator" in an otherwise standard-issue cafeteria brawl is absurd.

Online or Off—A Bully Is a Bully Is a Bully

Just as Facebook is not causing the death of genuine friendship, it is also not causing the birth of high school enemies. It only facilitates the malicious gossip, rumors, cruel insults and hormone-fueled anger that have long been a painful part of teenagers' lives. Yes, the use of social networking sites to make some kid's life miserable is troublesome—just like easily forwarded e-mails and texts, three-way calling, handwritten notes, and all the other public humiliation delivery systems of yore. And yes, the Internet's ability to expedite the destruction of a reputation, or the escalation of simmering tensions, is something parents need to make their kids aware of. But that doesn't mean blaming Facebook and strategizing to lure teenagers away from it. It means you have to start explaining to kids—ideally before they can type—that anything you post on the Internet has the potential to dog you *forever*; that secrets you text or e-mail to a friend, no matter how close, could be all over school (and, if they're interesting enough, the world) by morning; that talking smack online might just lead to a showdown in the cafeteria, etc. It means you have to acknowledge reality—these kids have already grown up online, and they'll be communicating via the Internet for the rest of their lives—instead of acting like social aggression never existed before Facebook, and there's still a chance that if we all wring our hands *really* hard, the genie might just go back in the bottle.

There Is No Going Back

Believe me, as a reasonably smart person who acquired both a painfully clichéd tattoo and a serious nicotine addiction at 17, I can appreciate the challenge of getting young people to grasp the long-term consequences of their behavior. But there's really no good alternative to *trying*. Claiming that "Facebook is the only common denominator" in an otherwise standard-issue (except perhaps for the fact that it was among girls) cafeteria brawl is absurd. To insist that social networking itself, as opposed to the vicious bullying it's used for, is responsible not only for incidents like the one at Scotch Plains-Fanwood High but for self-harm and suicides is to ignore all the kids who were pushed to the edge by whisper campaigns, passed notes and old-fashioned isolation long before home computers were common—and to continue sidestepping the underlying issue of social aggression. Facebook arguably makes it worse, but it certainly didn't create the problem. And since the Internet isn't going away anytime soon, the only option adults have is to try our best to prepare today's kids for the world they actually live in, not the one we vaguely remember.

6

Schoolchildren Are Not Ready for Social Networking

Kari Henley

Kari Henley is the president of the board of directors at the Women & Family Life Center in Guilford, Connecticut. She also organizes and facilitates the Association of Women Business Leaders and runs her own training and consulting practice.

While new Internet-based networking sites can be challenging for all users, children and teenagers might not yet have the maturity to use them properly, hurting friends and fellow students unintentionally. A child's brain does not have the capabilities to properly navigate the dangers of Facebook and MySpace, and parents need to be involved in their teenagers' social networking activities to ensure everyone's safety.

As a mother, I have recently discovered Facebook. My kids knew about it long ago and I poo pooed it as another mindless waste of time. Finally, I joined so I could track my kid's antics like a sneaky James Bond spy. Trouble is—I somehow got hooked myself. Suddenly, friends from far and wide started popping up. People from the dim recesses of my childhood resurfaced. Facebook is like a really good piece of chocolate or a bag of those great salt and vinegar potato chips.

However, the way I use Facebook is a bit different than the way my kids do, and plenty of kids are getting addicted beyond reason, using it for brutal cyber bullying or daring to say

Kari Henley, "Facebook and Kids: Are Their Brains Ready for Social Networking?" *Huffington Post*, March 22, 2009. Reproduced by permission of the author.

the types of things they would never dream of in person. Kids' depression rates are sky high, average onset at age 14, and there have been many reports of teen suicide from internet related bullying.

For over 25 million youth, Facebook is replacing email as "the" way to communicate, and parents are often left in the dust and wondering is it safe? What age can kids safely have a Facebook page? Should they [the parents] insist to be their "Friend" and monitor their endless chatter?

Jill is a mother of three children ages 10–14, who are fully into the digital generation. All have iPods, computers, Wii games, cell phones, and are addicted to Facebook. They are like most middle school aged kids in America today who have their hands on toys most adults only recently acquired themselves.

The Problem of Cyber Bullying

One day, a call came from the principal informing Jill and her husband, their middle daughter was being given in-school suspension for creating a Facebook group used to make fun of another student. Called something like, "*Eric is a Hairy Beast*," the group quickly filled with loads of kids making fun of a quiet Armenian boy, uploading cell phone pictures of him and becoming more brazen by the day.

> *For over 25 million youth, Facebook is replacing email as "the" way to communicate, and parents are often left in the dust and wondering is it safe?*

These kids are "A" students, and far from brats; but most are not cognitively developed enough to recognize their behavior is hurtful to others. According to Lisa Ott, the Youth Empowerment Coordinator at the Women and Family Life Center, this is on target with research in adolescent brain development.

Kids get into trouble with sites like Facebook and MySpace because they are too self-centered in their overall development to understand the impact of what they are doing, she said. Middle school age children are the most susceptible to cyber bullying, and high school students most likely to use poor judgment in giving out information.

Dr. Jay Giedd is the chief of brain imaging in the child psychiatry branch at the National Institute of Mental Health, and an expert in adolescent brain development. His research shows the brain is not fully developed at age 12 as was believed, but reaches full maturity in our mid-twenties. Adolescence is a time of profound brain development, surpassing that of toddlers. The area of the pre-frontal cortex develops last, which is in charge of higher reasoning and understanding consequences. The emotional centers of the brain that control happiness, fear, anger and sadness often over-compensate, and can be 50% stronger during adolescence.

I set about interviewing scores of parents with children from elementary to high school, asking their opinions about Facebook and kids. While most felt it was a relatively safe place for kids to connect to each other, many expressed concern over the obsessive nature of these sites. Designed to be "sticky;" a site is deemed successful the longer it entices you to stay on, yet these hours are replacing other activities critical for healthy development.

Most kids today don't have a local bowling alley or soda shop to hang out, like the baby boomer generations had.

A Critical Stage

A child's brain reaches its full size at age six and the gray matter is actually the thickest around age 12. Remember how the world was full of possibilities at that age? Because it truly is. After this stage, the brain begins to prune back gray matter and the phrase "use it or lose it" becomes key as certain brain cells die forever. The skills your child learns during adolescence; like sports, dancing, music or academics become hard wired. Other skills that are not being used will fall away. . . .

Most kids today don't have a local bowling alley or soda shop to hang out, like the baby boomer generations had. They also aren't allowed to play outside until the street lights come on as recent generations enjoyed. Hours of skipping rope, climbing trees and building forts is replaced with the tap tapping of tiny keyboards. The cyber playground has replaced the physical one, for better or worse. . . .

Peggy Orenstein, author of *Growing Up Daisy* recently wrote about "Growing Up on Facebook" in the *New York Times*. She notes most kids now going to college have been 'facebooking' since middle school, and wonders how our youth will be able to take the important steps of "reinventing themselves" with "450 friends watching, all tweeting to affirm ad nauseam your present self?"

Time will tell.

7

Social Networking Sites Can Be Hunting Grounds for Sexual Predators

John Kreiser

John Kreiser is a columnist and night editor at NHL.com, the Web site of the National Hockey League.

Sexual predators are using social networking sites to draw in teenagers to discuss sexually explicit material or meet them in person for sex. Because security on Facebook and MySpace is lax and the users' ages cannot be effectively verified, teenagers may face dangerous situations they are unable to navigate safely, and the outcomes could prove to be dire and sometimes even fatal.

It all started on the social networking Web site MySpace.com, reports CBS News correspondent Sandra Hughes. A 14-year-old girl began receiving graphic messages from a much older man, asking whether she was "OK with me being 38?"

It wasn't the first time the alleged predator, Robert Wise, trolled the Internet looking for sex, according to Sgt. Dan Krieger of the League City, Texas, police department.

"We assumed her online identity and started chatting with this guy," Krieger explains. "During that point, he made it very clear he wanted to meet her for sex. We were able to find another 14-year-old female that he's actually had sex with."

Wise is now in custody, charged with multiple counts of sexual assault.

John Kreiser, "MySpace: Your Kids' Danger," CBSNews.com, Feb. 6, 2006. Reproduced by permission.

But the incident is just one of many cases nationwide—and some of them have ended tragically.

Online Predators Are Dangerous

In New Jersey, Majalie Cajuste is grieving the murder of her daughter Judy. The 14-year-old reportedly told friends she met a man in his 20s through MySpace.com.

Across the country, in Northern California, friends are mourning 15-year-old Kayla Reed. She was active on MySpace until the day she disappeared.

[A]uthorities say many parents are clueless about their kids' MySpace profiles.

Police are investigating possible MySpace connections in both murder cases.

The Center for Missing and Exploited Children reported more than 2,600 incidents last year of adults using the Internet to entice children. With numbers like that, you'd think all parents would be hovering over their kids, wanting to know what they're doing online. But authorities say many parents are clueless about their kids' MySpace profiles.

CBS News Technology Analyst Larry Magid had a look at one personal profile on the site, belonging to a 15-year-old girl.

Magid says the girl writes in her description, "Drink a 40, smoke a bowl, sex is good, life is great, we are the class of 2008." . . .

In talking to some teens who regularly use MySpace, it's easy to see that a lot of kids aren't very careful about the information they put on their pages.

"So many people don't even use common sense," says Katie Pirtle, a high school student. "Some people even put their phone number on there."

Teenagers Do Not Worry About Online Predators

And while the information kids put on MySpace may be intended for their friends, do they think, "Hey there's 35-year-old or 45-year-old guys out there looking at my site?"

"Definitely not," says April Ehrlich, another high school student. "When they think MySpace, they think other teenagers. They don't think there are adults pretending to be teenagers on there."

The site requires users be 14 or older, and they are warned not to post any "personally identifiable material."

Many MySpace users post "the survey," which asks for responses about issues like drinking, drug use and skinny dipping. Users can also put up pictures.

MySpace declined CBS News' request for an on-camera interview but said in a statement: "We dedicate a third of our workforce to policing and monitoring our site."

The site requires users be 14 or older, and they are warned not to post any "personally identifiable material." But the teens we spoke to say that advice is routinely ignored.

"Just like a car accident, it can happen to you," says high school student Julia Rinaldi. "Predators can come to you—and that's what they don't think when they post those things."

Those predators include men like 26-year-old Jeffrey Neil Peters, who was arrested last month [January 2006] for sexually assaulting Susie Granger's daughter. Granger says parents should keep their kids off the site.

"Please don't allow your children to go onto MySpace," she says. "It's a very unsafe environment for them to be in."

But for the thousands of teens who are hooked on the site, it's a warning that's lost in cyberspace.

8

The Fear of Social Media Is Unfounded

Curtis Silver

Curtis Silver is a financial/data analyst and a contributor to Wired.com.

A common fear of Internet users is that social networking sites require them to share revealing personal information to everyone. However, Facebook and MySpace users can easily restrict access to their pages and freely choose what information to share and with whom. When used correctly, social networking sites are great tools to connect with friends and businesses alike and offer many advantages when looking for jobs or advertising your own business. Users need to gain knowledge and expertise to overcome their fear of social media, but the advantages LinkedIn, Facebook, or MySpace offer to participants far outweigh the possible risks.

When it comes to Social Media, a lot of individuals and companies are quite afraid. Fear of the unknown. Fear of lack of privacy. Fear of retribution and negative response. Fear of ex-girlfriends' new boyfriends, or of strangers stalking your kids. I hope to quell some of those fears with some good old fashioned rationalization and logical determination of what Social Media can do for you.

Social Media for Personal Use

When it comes to personal use, there is a lot more to fear from Social Media on an individual level than on a corporation level. There is a level of comfort that some were able to adapt to quickly (they all work in PR) and some took a little while longer to come around. Some still haven't come around, but have their little toes in the water and some flat out refuse to be involved at all. Most of the fear in the latter categories come from lack of knowledge about the Social Media networks and false assumptions about what kind of information you are required to share.

Let's talk about that for a moment. What information, on a personal level, are you required to share? That's actually a very simple answer, one that seems to elude many. None. You are required to share nothing. Plain and simple. I think this fear of being forced to provide personal data just because you signed up comes from cell phones. I'm serious. When cell phones became mainstream I remember people lamenting that now their friends and co-workers would be able to get hold of them wherever they were and an expectation was set that they would. That's the way the behavior drove the technology. Few people, if any, mentioned to me that the solution to that is to just not pick up the phone.

You are required to share nothing. Plain and simple.

It's the same thing for Social Media. You are only required to share as much information as you feel you should share. This is a fear I myself had to conquer when moving my persona onto Facebook. But then I realized that I can put whatever I want up there. I don't have to tell people my innermost secrets, I don't have to put my correct birthday or favorite foods. That's all optional. I don't even have to use my real name. The fear here is lack of privacy. People are afraid they will give away too much information. Well, only if you give away too much information. Again, at a personal level you aren't obligated to do anything at all, so it's completely up to you as to how you want to represent yourself online.

Privacy Can Be Maintained

When it came to more career oriented sites like Linkedin, the logic there was easier. What information would I be putting up on that site that wasn't already up on Monster.com or Careerbuilder? My resume, after being spread around the internet like herpes backstage at a rock concert, was pretty much public record. With that thought in mind, creating my profile on Linkedin was a walk in the park.

The other thing that really scares people, especially when it comes to networking sites, is connecting with the past. A lot of people have skeletons in the closet that they just don't want to let out. Or they don't want to be faced with the decision whether to "friend" an ex on Facebook or not. There is a lot of trepidation about what the expectation is when it comes to selecting your "friends" online. A great rule of thumb when it comes to that is—would you stop and talk to this person in real life? Is this someone you'd recognize in a crowded room? Someone you'd sit with uninvited at a coffee shop if you knew them? I have acquaintances from high school that try to connect with me on Facebook, but I either A.) didn't like them then and probably wouldn't like them now or B.) have no freaking clue who they are. Why should I feel obligated to connect? Am I that self centered to think that if I don't connect they are brooding over it? Chances are, I'm one of a hundred invites they sent out that day.

I spoke to a friend who is consumed by the fear. The media hasn't helped, with stories of MySpace & Facebook predators and so on. That's where his fear stems from—he's afraid his family would be targeted. It may be a harsh conclusion, but you may as well never leave the house and never let your family out of the house as well. It's a rough and tumble world out there, and even more so online. You have to have a particular constitution about you and be armed with the knowledge of what's out there and what kind of programs you are working with. The fact that Linkedin pulled in his gmail account address book scared the crap out of him. You can't be participating online with that glaring lack of knowledge about how the internet and its related applications work. Arm yourself with knowledge and the fear will subside.

The other thing that really scares people, especially when it comes to networking sites, is connecting with the past.

Knowledge Is Key to Social Networking

Getting over these fears are tough. However, they are clearly worth the benefits. I have several thousand connections on Linkedin, people I don't know in industries I've never heard of—but they are there. Ready and mostly willing to provide information and insight when needed. I've made advantageous connections on Facebook with people I've not seen in years, working for or running businesses that could benefit my life. I've connected with people outside my zip code—which is the most important part. I've gotten freelance jobs through connections, been involved in projects I never would have known about had I not been connected. With networks like Twitter, I've got a constant stream of what's going on in the world and with subjects I'm interested in. Not to mention the quick availability to self promote via utilities like Digg. Those are the benefits. . . .

Social Media for Business Use

With business use, whether it be to self promote or promote your business, there are different fears but based on the same inherent base fears. Lack of knowledge is the big one, followed by general apathy and ignorance. Businesses don't worry about the privacy issue as much as an individual would.

What they do worry about is the return on investment. Is Social Media worth the time and effort? Based on Social Media consulting being a whole sub-industry of public relations,

I'd say many companies think it is worth the time and effort. Basically, companies need to ask themselves if they have the time and resources to commit to networking. If they don't, then it's a moot point and less of a fear of using Social Media than an apathetic response.

The bigger question for companies or individuals looking to self promote, is do their customers use it? For me, the answer was a hearty "yes." As a writer, joining Twitter was one of the best ways to promote my own work. Did I mention that you can follow me? See? Self promotion.

I've made advantageous connections on Facebook with people I've not seen in years, working for or running businesses that could benefit my life.

Businesses hire Social Media experts to guide them onto the internet and promote their service and/or product. This is especially useful if a good percentage of their customer base is deeply rooted in the social networks. More companies are adding a Twitter feed to their contact page, or their CEO suddenly has his own blog to rant on.

A fear here is feedback. A lot of companies are flat out terrified of negative feedback. Terrified. Like walking in the dark and likely be eaten by a Grue [fictional predator] terrified. However, that suggests something exists that would cause negative feedback. A good key for any company using Social Media is honesty and clarity with customers and consumers. If you have something to hide and it's revealed, there will be negative feedback. In any forum however, there will always be negative feedback. Have you ever read the op-ed section of the newspaper?

There Is Money in Social Networking

Businesses can benefit the most from Social Media, more than any personal usage outside of self-promotion. Because there is money to be made. How is there money to be made? It's basic economics. Reach a larger audience, sell more product/service and make more money. There are companies that wouldn't exist right now if not for Social Media. Independents based online are thriving because of the networking possibilities of Social Media. As are Social Media consulting firms. Self promotion is another great side benefit as well. Can you think of how you would self promote a blog post before Social Media? Email everyone? That limits you to people you know. Send them certified mail?

In conclusion, and to sum it all up nicely (especially the part about using common sense), a quote from Boston based branding and PR Executive Don Martelli:

> The social media fear factor is real, but controllable. Rather than being scared of eating bugs and goat intestines, the fear factor—personally and professionally—is really embedded in one thing, engagement. People are nervous of connecting with past lives and sharing stuff that they care not to. Brands are nervous about the two way communication street that social channels pave, especially with those on the road that aren't kind.
>
> Whether from a personal or professional standpoint, the fear factor can be controlled by using common sense and being transparent in your communications. My advice is to leverage the reach of social media to become a trusted source of helpful content, which, in turn, will help companies and their brands build a following or stronger community.

9

Social Networking Sites Are Increasingly Frequented by Stalkers

National Center for Victims of Crime

The National Center for Victims of Crime is a resource and advocacy organization for crime victims and those who serve them. Its mission is to help victims of crime rebuild their lives and to serve individuals, families, and communities harmed by crime.

Social networking sites are increasingly used by online predators and other criminals to stalk their prey. They post hateful messages, track their victims' whereabouts, and set up pages solely to harass and slander others. While the law is starting to catch up with new forms of stalking, a person's best defense is to keep private information safe from unwanted intruders, to use the site's privacy settings, and to investigate so-called "friends" before allowing them access to one's site.

"Vengeance will be mine . . . ," declared a defiant message on MySpace.com. "I should have killed you all when I had a gun and some drugs." This violent monologue, one of several postings on the writer's site, threatened his ex-wife, who had fled the state to escape his abuse. In postings on other sites, he demanded photos of his family and warned that if he didn't get to see the kids, "it isn't going to be real good, because I'm gonna see them whether you let me or not."

National Center for Victims of Crime, "Social Networking Sites: A Bonanza for Stalkers?" 2007. Reproduced by permission.

The increasing use of MySpace to threaten and stalk victims raises many important questions. Do social networking sites enable stalking? What recourse do victims have when these sites are used to stalk? And what tools can help block the use of these sites to stalk?

The Rise of Social Networking Sites

Social networking sites such as MySpace and Facebook are virtual communities where people with mutual interests meet on-line to share information and build relationships. Site visitors can chat, debate, network, and socialize. On many sites, members may post details about themselves—photos; educational backgrounds; favorite books, movies, and music; and relationship status. Other sites promote business, activism, networking, counseling, socializing, or many types of recreational interests. Sites such as MySpace, Facebook, Friendster, and Xanga have attracted millions of members, particularly among teenagers and young adults.

On many social networking sites, anyone with a computer and Internet access can become a member. Some sites require only an e-mail address, and many sites have no system to verify the validity of information that registrants provide. A few sites, including MySpace and Friendster, have minimum age requirements (14 and 16, respectively) although these sites have no reliable method to verify a user's age. Once a member, anyone can post personal information, images, music, or other data on their Web pages, depending on the site's features. On many sites, members select a circle of "friends" who can post messages on their profiles, add comments, or access pages not visible to other users. Unless the site allows members to control access to specific information (and members actually exercise those options), everything posted on a profile may be visible to all site visitors. Most sites require members to agree to terms of proper conduct, but enforcement of such terms is sporadic and often depends on members to report violations.

loaded, spyware can help stalkers gather information about all their victims' computer activity, including e-mails, chats, instant messages, keystrokes, passwords, and Web sites visited.

Legal Recourse

Stalkers who use social networking sites as part of a pattern of stalking may be subject to criminal charges. For example, someone who repeatedly follows and tracks a victim in her car, as well as posts a lewd photo of the victim on a social networking site, can be charged with the crime of stalking. Also in many states, cyberstalking statutes enable prosecutors to charge those who use technology to stalk and harass their victims. Other states have general stalking laws that define "pattern of conduct" broadly enough to cover the use of technology to stalk. Most of these laws are relatively new, however, and few cases involving social networking sites have yet been prosecuted.

Stalkers who use social networking sites as part of a pattern of stalking may be subject to criminal charges.

Victims also have options in civil or family courts. They can seek protective orders against stalkers, who can be ordered not to contact the victim, including not using any form of electronic communications to stalk the victim. Victims may also be able to file a civil tort case against their stalker, seeking damages for the impact of stalking on their lives. Also, under certain conditions, victims can sue social networking sites for failure to remove offensive or defamatory material regarding the victim from the site.

Lawmakers are starting to propose measures to govern the use of social networking sites. In April 2007, for example, the California legislature introduced a bill to prevent individuals from using social networking sites to incite harassment or abuse against an individual. Harassment would include posting digital images or messages on Web sites to cause fear, harassment, or harm to an individual.

The Best Defense Is Prevention

The best defense against social networking site stalking is to use the sites with extreme caution. Wise users carefully consider what they post. Last names, school names, favorite hangouts, phone numbers, and addresses make it easy for stalkers to locate victims. Photos with identifiers (like school names or locations) also increase a victim's vulnerability. Posted information is permanently public. "You can't take it back," warn experts Larry Magid and Anne Collier, about information posted on-line. "Deleted" information can be recovered, for example, from Google's cache of deleted and changed Web pages and from Internet Archive (*archive.org*), which offers access to deleted postings.

Users can also boost security by limiting on-line "friends" to people they actually know and by activating all available privacy settings. Since June 2006, MySpace has allowed all users to keep their profiles private—open only to those designated as "friends." MySpace also offers other privacy options: to control how others may add their names to friends lists, to approve friends' comments before posting, to hide the feature that shows when they are on-line, or to prevent e-mailing photos. To activate these features, members must change their settings and choose the privacy options they prefer. Although stalkers can find ways around these protections, members who use them are less vulnerable than those who do not.

The social networking revolution presents complex dilemmas. The convenience and appeal of these sites are undeniable, and stalking cases that involve social networking are still quite rare. Yet as stalkers diversify their tactics, they are likely to exploit any available technology. For stalking victims as well as the public, safe social networking will require awareness and vigilance.

10

Social Networking Sites Are Addictive

Sam Leith

Sam Leith was the Daily Telegraph's *literary editor for about ten years and is a frequent contributor to a variety of British newspapers and magazines.*

Facebook, which lets you check on your friends' updates and largely irrelevant likes and dislikes, has the same addictive qualities possessed by illegal drugs. Although seemingly less harmful, Facebook occupies office workers' minds incessantly and causes a drop in productivity and creativity among them.

"Matthew d'Ancona," the email said, "added you as a friend on Facebook. We need you to confirm that you are, in fact, friends with Matthew." ROTFLMAO, as we say on the internet. Even the editor of *The Spectator* has now joined Facebook.

Like many adult crazes, Facebook is for children: a "social networking" website where you post photos, dig up your fave pop stars, and, through the links to other people's pages, snoop around stalking your exes and spying on your friends.

It is, unfortunately, addictive. (Addiction is much on my mind these days, largely because having given up cigarettes and alcopops, I've got far too much time to think.) But it's an odd addiction.

Consider the ordinary lab-rat, once taught that pressing a lever will give him a rat-sized hit of crack. The little fellow, according to scientists, gazes around himself at the circumstances of his confinement and thinks, like a rat Tony Hancock: stone me, what a life.

Any moderately computer-literate lab-rat knows it's pretty straightforward to email someone and wait for them to reply.

And, in nine out of 10 double-blind control-group-normalised peer-reviewed studies, he paws that lever like a performing horse asked to calculate the ratio between the circumference of a circle and its diameter. He self-medicates until he is but a fistful of bones in a threadbare fur coat. This rat, I can identify with. Until recently he could, I fancy, identify with me. But Facebook is an addiction ole Ratty would look on with pity and contempt.

Any moderately computer-literate lab-rat knows it's pretty straightforward to email someone and wait for them to reply. Comparatively less straightforward is to log in to Facebook, send them a message through Facebook, wait for Facebook to email them advising them that they have a message from you that they must log in to Facebook to collect, then wait for the email from Facebook advising you that they have replied to your message, then log in to Facebook to collect their reply. (The fact that that sentence contains six mentions of the word "Facebook" is one clue as to why the service is provided for free.)

Then there's the "News Feed". Facebook is the Reuters of irrelevance, the AFP of inanity. Look at it now. The "top news line", as we call it in the trade, is that at 10:51, Larushka Ivan-Zadeh became "undecided". Just three minutes before that, Toby Young added *Rio Bravo* to his list of favourite movies. Mo Kanneh, I discover, became "chill" at 11:59pm, 3:01am, and 5:04am. Presumably he now resembles a fish-finger after a big night out in Aberdeen. Update! 11:11am: Ben Price removed *Dirty Harry* from his list of favourite movies.

Ratty, baffled, looks up at me, his eyes goggling. Yet there I sit, pawing F5 to refresh the page with a regularity that reminds me of, well, a performing horse. I don't feel like a cigarette. I barely feel like a drink. I am wallowing in trivia, along with millions of others. In the process, all who hate the sinister growth of the surveillance society, who value privacy and deplore the seep of personal data into the aquifers of government and the marketing industries, are voluntarily surrendering ourselves to self-surveillance. All for no more than the odd poke (Facebook jargon—take it on trust) from nice Matt d'Ancona.

Facebook's administrators have access to a database about who knows who, how they know them, their sexual behaviour, favourite movies and what time they are chill: a database of which the Stasi or the Mukhabarat could only have dreamed. We must hope it won't find its way to the marketing men or—through some emergency arrogation of powers—the security services.

Sooner or later, privacy be damned, the damage Facebook causes to the British economy in lost productivity may have to be offset by the sale of its data to marketing companies.

We must more than hope it won't make its way to our employers. I mean, I don't wish to tell tales, but I couldn't help noticing the editor of *The Spectator* tinkering with his favourite films during office hours on Thursday, and yesterday, nine minutes before midday, joining the group "Hey Ho Let's Go! The Ramones."

I'm one to talk. Facebook made me so neglect my work on Wednesday that I caused a colleague to have a stress-related asthma attack. Sooner or later, privacy be damned, the damage Facebook causes to the British economy in lost productivity may have to be offset by the sale of its data to marketing companies.

It is, in other words, a colossal and pernicious waste of time. You know what to do. ALT-F4. Close down your computer. Buy a pack of fags [cigarettes]. And go to the pub for a treble vodka and a bit of what we might call Facetime with our old pal Ratty.

11

Social Networking Sites Give Users an Inflated Sense of Self

Debra Ronca

Debra Ronca is a content developer, writer, and editor. She is an expert on pop culture and writes television commentary and interviews with industry insiders and celebrities.

While social networking addiction is not yet a clinical term, many users display symptoms similar to those of drug users. Social networking is nothing new, but the Internet allows us to network around the clock and create virtual personalities. It also allows us to spy on our friends and follow them in a voyeuristic manner. Without any real-world barriers—distance, appropriate times, money—social networking sites create the illusion of importance and flatter the narcissist in everyone.

In April 2009, Oprah Winfrey logged on to Twitter and sent her first "tweet," taking online social networking out of the hands of the computer-savvy and into the living rooms of every American. These days it seems like everyone and their grandma has a Facebook page, Twitter account or LinkedIn profile. People are logging on every day, obsessively updating their profiles and checking the status updates of their online friends. It's a fun way to pass the time and stay in touch, but can these sites be dangerous? Can you become addicted to social networking?

Social networking is not a new concept. In fact, it's been around as long as we have. A social network is simply the

Debra Ronca, "Are Social Networking Sites Addictive?" HowStuffWorks.com, 2009. Reproduced by permission.

structure of relationships among individuals. Everyone on the planet is part of one big social network, but we also belong to smaller, more distinct subnetworks. We define these subnetworks by criteria like our families, friends, jobs, schools, hobbies and more. You have a social network at work. You have a social network at the dog park by your house. You have a social network with your college friends. You have a social network with your Tuesday night book club. The list goes on and on, and many people in your network may overlap. Additionally, your contacts multiply all the time, as you meet new people through the people in your existing networks.

These days it seems like everyone and their grandma has a Facebook page, Twitter account or LinkedIn profile.

Networking in Cyberspace

Social networking Web sites evolved from these face-to-face networks. The online sites, though, are powerful because they harness the strength of the Internet to manage and map out your relationships. You can physically see your network—your friends, your friends' friends, and so on—and how you connect with all of them.

Social networking sites allow people to manage their relationships as well as find new ones. Some communities, such as LinkedIn, target professionals. Some, such as the crochet/ knitting community Ravelry, target people with specific hobbies. And some, such as Facebook or MySpace, are general interest community sites that allow users to form smaller communities within.

Once you join a social networking site, you may find yourself spending a lot of time there. Is it all in good fun, or can online social networks be addictive?

Internet Addiction

Today's kids spend a lot of time in front of digital screens. A 2007 study from the University of Southern California's Annenberg School Center for the Digital Future showed that almost half of all parents surveyed believed their kids spent too much time watching television, and 20.7 percent felt their kids spent too much time online.

A 20 percent concern about online engagement is relatively low. But that doesn't mean there aren't problems. For example, in 2005, a young South Korean man actually collapsed and died after playing online for 50 hours with few breaks. Concerned authorities even founded "Internet Rescue Schools" to get children away from their computers and into fresh air, physical activity and socializing with other kids.

Children aren't the only ones who can get hooked on the Internet. In 2008, the *American Journal of Psychiatry* published an editorial in support of naming "Internet addiction" as a bona fide mental condition. The majority of the medical community disagreed, though, and currently Internet addiction is not a formal disorder. However, excessive use of the Internet can certainly cause problems.

Even though it's not formally classified, many treatment and rehab centers worldwide now offer services for Internet addiction. This includes treatment for cyberporn, online gambling, online affairs and eBay addiction. Of course, these are all behaviors with serious consequences. The hallmark of an addiction is determining whether your actions are affecting yourself or others in a negative way.

So, is hanging out on Facebook any different from talking on the phone for hours, or gabbing with your friends over coffee? Not if you're spending normal amounts of time there. The average American Internet user spends about 15 hours online per month. If you're reading this article, then more than likely, you're one of those people. Congratulations! You're average!

However, if you're spending abnormally large amounts of time online, you could be damaging your relationships and even your health. Experts claim that a lack of face-to-face contact can affect you both socially and physically. Depending upon a computer screen for human interaction might undermine the ability to follow social cues or understand body language. In addition, some researchers believe that we're genetically predisposed to physically benefit from being face-to-face with another human. There's even an online test you can take to see if the time you spend online might be a problem (unless you're addicted to online tests, of course).

[I]n 2005, a young South Korean man actually collapsed and died after playing online for 50 hours with few breaks.

If you're one of the many who belong to a social network, you've had a taste of how addicting these Web sites can be. What is it that compels us to keep logging on?

Addictive by Design

Web sites are a product, and any product pusher wants return customers. When more visitors keep returning to a site, it means more ad revenue. And more ad revenue means more money for the company that owns the site. Programmers design every element on a social networking site to suck you in and keep you coming back.

How do they do this? Sites like Twitter and Facebook offer "status updates" where users can enter a few short phrases about what they're doing at that very moment. Users may find themselves constantly checking their friends' updates, or changing their own updates on a regular basis. If you comment on someone else's photo or update, sites will generate an email to let you know. You can reach out and "poke" a friend, take a quiz or survey and compare the results with your friends or upload a photo of your new puppy doing something cute so everyone can ooh and ahh over him. You reach out to the site and it reaches out to you—keeping you coming back from a few to a few dozen times a day.

With the increasing popularity of wireless devices like the BlackBerry or iPhone—devices that can move lots of data very quickly—users have access to their social networks 24 hours a day. Most social networking sites have developed applications for your mobile phone, so logging on is always convenient. Social networks also tap into our human desire to stay connected with others. The rush of nostalgia as you connect with your former grade-school classmate on Facebook can be quite heady and exciting.

Web sites are a product, and any product pusher wants return customers. When more visitors keep returning to a site, it means more ad revenue.

A Case of Narcissism

But what's the main reason we find these sites so addictive? Plain old narcissism. We broadcast our personalities online whenever we publish a thought, photo, YouTube video or answer one of those "25 Things About Me" memes. We put that information out there so people will respond and connect to us. Being part of a social network is sort of like having your own entourage that follows you everywhere, commenting on and applauding everything you do. It's very seductive.

In 2008, researchers at the University of Georgia studied the correlation between narcissism and Facebook users. Unsurprisingly, they found that the more "friends" and wall posts a user had, the more narcissistic he or she was. They noted that narcissistic people use Facebook in a self-promoting way, rather than in a connective way. It may be an obvious theory, but it also suggests that social networks bring out the narcissist in all of us.

Social networks are also a voyeuristic experience for many users. Following exchanges on Twitter or posts on Facebook and MySpace are akin to eavesdropping on someone else's conversation. It's entertaining and allows you to feel like a "fly on the wall" in someone else's life.

Social networking sites also publicly list your "friends" or "followers"—giving you instant status. How many people do you know online who spend all their time trying to get more friends, more followers, more testimonials? We work hard in real life to elevate our statuses, make friends and search out boosters for our self-esteem. Online social networking provides this to us, and we don't even have to change out of our sweatpants to get it.

12

Students Admitted Early to College Network on Facebook

Jenna Johnson

Jenna Johnson is a Student Life and Culture reporter at the Washington Post.

To help students make the transition from high school to college life, many universities set up Facebook sites for incoming classes. These allow future students to get to know each other and get involved in campus activities long before classes begin. While many of the friendships might not endure, these Facebook pages take the bite out of finding one's way around a new school and city.

The first 570 members of George Washington University's Class of 2014 found out they had been accepted one day in early December. Within hours, they began to network on Facebook—making friends, debating dorms, discussing "Real World: Washington D.C." and organizing a Wiffle ball team.

"Let the friend requests begin lol. Congrats again guys, 2014 all the way!" a high school senior from New Jersey posted late that night. A few days later, a senior from Illinois wrote, "The senioritis has definitely begun."

College classes don't start for eight months, senior year of high school is barely half over and most deadlines for general admission still haven't hit, but students who committed to attending selective universities through early decision programs have gotten a jump on their virtual college life.

"I already have a sense of having a class of close-knit friends," said Ryan Counihan, a high school senior from Boston who turned 18 last week and received online birthday wishes from several future GWU classmates. "We definitely have a leg up.... We have an extra four months or so to get to know each other."

At several colleges across the country, early decision has become an online clique, an opportunity to become a leader at a school they do not yet attend. The University of Chicago Class of 2014 Facebook group proclaims: "Well, we've gotten a head start on everything else. Let's meet each other!" A group at Brown University boasts, "The rest of the masses will find out if they'll be joining us early April."

GWU has a half-dozen Class of 2014 groups on Facebook, and the largest has more than 325 members. (Anyone can join, and there is no guarantee that all members have been accepted.) Together, the students have watched the mail for their acceptance packages, compared financial aid offerings, debated the pros and cons of living in a dorm known for having a "party culture," and marveled at how cool it will be to live in the District.

At several colleges across the country, early decision has become an online clique, an opportunity to become a leader at a school they do not yet attend.

"Umm we'll be in DC for the next presidential inauguration ... WHAT," a girl from New York posted. Fourteen others hit the "like" button, and a girl from Chicago responded, "I was thinking about that today and freaked out ahhh!"

And there are plans for non-virtual contact: More than 60 students in the New York area will meet this month or next, and a smaller group in Boston will do the same. A handful of Chicago students met last month.

Students who apply for early decision tend to be devoted fans of the school, said Steve Roche, director of GWU's freshman orientation program, Colonial Inauguration. And that makes them more likely to plunge into networking once they are accepted.

Being accepted into college begins the transition from high school, Roche said, and often a Facebook profile metamorphosis: Besides adding friends and joining college networks, students might remove prom photos and ditch their loyalty to the Jonas Brothers.

Going through that transition in the middle of senior year, rather than right before graduation or over the summer, can be jarring. So when students or their parents called Roche last week asking for orientation information, he gently told them: "Here's the information. But worry about your high school career.... It's December, heading into January. Don't forget that you have that extra semester."

But for many students, the carefully choreographed college admissions process is starting sooner in their high school careers. Early decision, which is used by competitive colleges to fill part of their freshman class months ahead of time, has become more popular in recent years.

Going through that transition in the middle of senior year, rather than right before graduation or over the summer, can be jarring.

GWU received 70 percent more early decision applications this fall than two years ago. The university is holding a second early decision round this month. The deadline for that and general admission is Jan. 10.

Occasionally, the early deciders remind each other that they aren't the only members of the Class of 2014—and that others will quickly join the groups they've set up. The real test of their Facebook friendships will come when they meet each other.

These days, students increasingly come to freshman orientation knowing 30 or 40 people rather than being just vaguely acquainted with their roommate from the awkward phone call in which they decide who is bringing the microwave, Roche said. Still, most of those Facebook-forged friendships won't last.

"It's good because it makes them feel more comfortable," Roche said. "Just in my experience, those friendships don't last more than a week or two into the semester."

Max Hoffman, 17, broadcast the news of his acceptance on GWU's main Facebook page but has resisted joining the Class of 2014 group, friending future classmates or replying to the guy who wants to be his roommate.

"I don't want to push the whole process," said Hoffman, who lives outside of Boston. "I want to enjoy high school."

13

Social Spam Is Pervasive

Chris Wilson

Chris Wilson is an associate editor at the online magazine Slate *in Washington, D.C.*

Spam is a nuisance for anyone who uses e-mail, but new programs and viruses from what appear to be social networking sites can infiltrate your list of contacts and send all your friends or business associates unwanted messages. In order to keep accounts safe from abuse, users need to surf safely and change passwords frequently.

Until last weekend, I had never heard of WeGame.com, the go-to source for videos of video games. Then, on Sunday, I got an e-mail from a casual acquaintance with the subject line "[casual acquaintance] has sent you a photo!" Naturally, I clicked the link, which took me to WeGame. The site invited me to see this photo—just as soon as I entered my e-mail password, which it promised not to remember.

The site's tactic is dirty and obvious: When you give it your login info, it mines all the contacts from your account and fires off an identical e-mail to all of them with your name in the subject line. I got several more WeGame messages on both my Gmail and work accounts from infrequent contacts, like the friend of an ex-girlfriend's current boyfriend. There's nothing truly evil going on here—it appears to just be an overzealous publicity campaign on WeGame's part. This episode of "social spamming," however, does reveal a ripe oppor-

Chris Wilson, "Your Gullible Friend Has Sent You a Photo!" *Slate*, Sept. 23, 2009. Reproduced by permission.

tunity for more pernicious spammers to get access to your accounts and cause all sorts of trouble.

Social Spamming Is Pervasive

There are times when it's useful to allow a Web site to peek at your contacts list. Both Facebook and Twitter offer to search your e-mail to find friends' profiles or user names. WeGame, which is a serious project that raised $3 million when it launched, has as much right as anyone to market itself to users' friends via e-mail. The difference is that WeGame encourages you actually to *send mail* to all your contacts, firing out misleading messages if you click "yes" too many times without reading carefully. Every time I logged in, the photo my friend allegedly wanted to share was the same: a picture of two people dressed as the Mario Bros.

Not only were victims hacked; all of their friends knew they were gullible.

I signed up on WeGame with a dummy account on Monday morning to see exactly how easy it is to spam all your friends accidentally. Once I went through the sign-up process, I got to a pop-up that asked me to "confirm [my] e-mail invites." All of the contacts in my dummy account's address book were selected. In order to avoid spamming everyone, I had to hit cancel and start unchecking names. This actually represents progress for the site. Armin Rosen, a Columbia University senior who fell for the WeGame scheme, tells me that he "didn't even see the list of e-mails" he was about to send when he signed up. (In response to my questions about his site's publicity strategies, WeGame founder Jared Kim pleaded ignorance, telling me only that his "team makes pretty rapid changes" to WeGame's functionality.)

I can't remember the last time I saw any piece of old-school spam that looked believable. The spelling and grammar are often hopelessly mangled, and we've all learned not to open weird attachments or send strangers our bank account information. But notes like the one from WeGame are a new breed. Because we are so accustomed to interacting with friends over social networking sites, getting an e-mail about a photo link doesn't seem strange. Sites that pose as social networks are the new spammers, and they're a lot harder to sniff out than the traditional penis enlargement and fake Rolex watch crowd.

Paying a High Price

Consider the case of ViddyHo.com. The site, which launched in February [2009], promised you a video if you logged in through MSN Messenger, AIM, or Gmail, among other sites. This isn't such a strange request. Facebook Connect allows other Web purveyors to use Facebook profiles as a form of identification, and your Gmail password is your ticket to all of Google's tools and gadgets. ViddyHo wasn't on the level, though, and people who fell for the trick paid the price. If you handed over your Gmail username and password, the site proceeded to GChat all of your friends to spread the good news about ViddyHo. Not only were victims hacked; all of their friends knew they were gullible.

The damage caused by ViddyHo, as with WeGame, appears limited to embarrassment. Hoan Ton-That, the site's San Francisco-based creator, told me in April that he didn't mean to auto-invite people's entire address books, though the fact that he has a new site with similar ambitions is not heartening. But there's nothing preventing the next ViddyHo from doing more damage, logging passwords and contacts for more sinister purposes.

Like any good scam, social spam exploits our trust—the belief that our friends wouldn't invite us to join a site with bad intentions. Versions of this trick have been around since the height of AOL Instant Messenger's dominance, when I would occasionally get IMs from friends with purported links to articles about Osama Bin Laden's capture. (I clicked on that one.) But the rise of social networking has made these scams even more convincing. I have a feeling most of the victims of the WeGame e-mails were more absent-minded than gullible. We decide we're going to register for some new site and then go into autopilot, typing in whatever we're asked for in the fields. After all, we've done it a thousand times before without incident. (One victim at Wesleyan claims to have been on the phone while absently clicking through the motions and ended up infecting her best friend's mother.)

Think twice whenever a site asks for your Webmail password.

The Dangers Are Real

It's easy to imagine how social spam could wreak real havoc. Imagine a site—vouched for in a friend's e-mail message, naturally—that asks users to provide their e-mail address as a login, then prompts them to set up a password. It would then be elementary for the wicked Web site to check whether this e-mail/password combo opens the user's Webmail account. Considering how often people use the same password for all of their Web transactions, I bet that simple scheme would work a lot of the time. Once the Webmail has been cracked, the wicked Web site could send invitations to everyone in the contact list—and plunder the inbox for valuable goodies like bank account information or Social Security numbers.

If WeGame and its ilk continue to proliferate, it may fall to the Webmail clients to place extra protections on how outside sites can mine contacts. "We don't approve of third-party sites handling their users' information in this way," a Google spokesperson told me, adding that "in some cases we may take more proactive measures to identify and block the spam."

WeGame doesn't actually send mail from users' Gmail accounts—it just sends all your contacts e-mail with your name in the subject line. On account of that, the best Google could have done immediately would have been to block e-mail that came from WeGame. In the meantime, a quick, finger-wagging PSA: The rise of social spam is yet another reason to practice safe surfing. Think twice whenever a site asks for your Web-mail password. And for the millionth time, don't use the same password for everything.

14

Pro-Anorexia Sites Should Be Banned

Sarah Menkedick

Sarah Menkedick is a writer and editor. Her work has been published in Literary Traveler, Abroad View Magazine, *and* National Geographic Glimpse, *among others. She is a contributing editor at* Matador Abroad, *and she blogs about women's rights for Change.org.*

While censorship is rarely justified and often harms more than it helps, in the face of Web sites advertising an anorexic "lifestyle," drastic action is necessary. These sites are harmful not only to unsuspecting teenagers surfing the Internet but also to victims of anorexia nervosa, who, seeking help for their disorder, discover sites that proclaim to help afflicted girls but instead endorse starvation. Pro-anorexia Web sites need to be shut down to keep teenage girls safe from their damaging influence.

Last year [2009], France's lower house passed a bill that would make pro-anorexia (pro-Ana) websites illegal. Valerie Boyer, the center-right parliament member who introduced the bill, said that she does not want the websites' "perverse and morbid" tips, which ultimately lead to death, seen by children. (In France, anorexia occurs predominantly in girls between 12 and 13 and 18 and 19.)

Sarah Menkedick, "Should Pro-Anorexia Websites Be Banned?" Change.org., January 11, 2010. Reproduced by permission.

France's health minister, Roselyne Bachelot, backed the law, arguing that giving young women advice on how to starve and torture themselves and avoid parents and doctors does not fall under freedom of expression.

For the women who create and follow pro-Ana sites, anorexia is not simply a disease, it is a code, an oath they take with one another, a way of life.

Lawmakers Should Intervene

In general, I am wary of any government legislation criminalizing bloggers, and worse, punishing women for discussing illnesses related to body image. However, reading some of the pro-Ana sites (the photos on "thinspiration" sites . . . were particularly disturbing) pushed me into an unlikely point of view: I fully support the measures taken in France.

For the women who create and follow pro-Ana sites, anorexia is not simply a disease, it is a code, an oath they take with one another, a way of life. They set themselves in opposition to anyone who is not part of the Ana community. One blogger, who had just emerged from a recovery program that her concerned friends and family sent her to, wrote about how great it was to be back in the community and encouraged readers to join her in a thirty hour fast. The post's 64 comments weighed in with guilt over having eaten too much or not fasted enough and professed solidarity with the blogger.

If one blogger can be forcibly removed from her life and sent to a clinic, and then return to inspire her followers on a thirty-hour fast, how can we expect people addicted to pro-Ana sites to recover?

While the bill is currently stewing in the French Senate, people have been weighing in on its proposed effects and consequences. Ars Technica labels the law "counterproductive" and, incredibly, compares pro-Ana sites to those advertising bacon cheeseburgers, asking if all websites potentially construed as dangerous could in the future be legislated against. Meanwhile, the documentary *Arresting Ana* stresses that the law punishes women who are looking for salvation in "Ana," the mythical representation of anorexia who to them is a friend, confidante, and kind of "guru." *Arresting Ana* seems to believe that turning these women into criminals will not only leave them with a jail sentence and a fine, but also take away their reason for living.

The incredibly destructive nature of these pro-Ana communities—and the way they encourage girls as young as 12 and 13 to hide their illnesses and to continue starving themselves—demands action.

Goodwill Is Not Enough

The French fashion industry has also voiced its displeasure. Enlightened designer Jean-Paul Gaultier claimed that anorexia is a problem solved not by laws, but by understanding. Well thank you, Jean-Paul. The hollow cheeks and shrunken stomachs of your models are demonstrating an understanding of what, exactly? The direct relationship between fashion and extreme thinness? Ah, right. Guess we don't need laws, then, when we've got your "understanding."

The incredibly destructive nature of these pro-Ana communities—and the way they encourage girls as young as 12 and 13 to hide their illnesses and to continue starving themselves—demands action. Not only laws, of course; also society-wide efforts to combat the notion that extreme thinness is desirable and beautiful, and resources and positive support groups for women struggling with body image.

Quite simply, I wonder how possible it is to help anorexic women if they can constantly run from parents, friends, and professional help into the arms of a community that encourages them to never give up, and to never to eat more than 800 calories a day.

15

Pro-Anorexia Sites Should Not Be Banned

Angie Rankman

Angie Rankman writes about contemporary women's issues and is a contributor to Aphrodite Women's Health.

Despite the disturbing content of pro-anorexia sites, which advocate an unhealthy lifestyle and starvation, censorship is not the right answer. Instead of driving the "pro-ana" movement underground, where it will still prey on teenagers with eating disorders, it is safer to allow "pro-ana" sites and study the affliction and people involved with the movement. Treating anorexia nervosa is a difficult task at best, and disallowing Web sites that deal with the many facets of the disorder deprives researchers of valuable material. To render pro-ana supporters invisible should not be confused with helping afflicted teenagers and women.

It has been argued that the Internet is a democratic, equalizing force within society, and the plethora of views and opinions on personal websites perhaps reinforces that idea. But with the proliferation of porn and file sharing sites, democracy and free speech have had their limits tested. And pushing the envelope with the best (and worst) of them is the pro-anorexic social movement called "pro-ana". A rapid decline in the visibility of pro-ana sites on the Internet may be vindication enough for those in favor of censoring pro-ana sites, but a question mark hangs over the censorship of the online pro-ana movement. Yes, the sites might well be away from view, but is it a case of out-of-sight out-of-mind?

Angie Rankman, "Pro-Ana: Still Dying to Be Thin," *Aphrodite Women's Health*, June 12, 2006. Reproduced by permission.

Starving by Choice

Pro-ana is a social movement among girls (mostly) who use websites, forums and blogs to advocate the idea that anorexia is a *lifestyle* choice rather than a disorder. The pro-ana sites are filled with forums and discussion boards targeting girls who share the same philosophy. Pro-ana sites portray thin celebrities (dubbed "thinspirations") such as Paris Hilton, Angelina Jolie and Kate Moss as role models; and links to other sites such as *Skinny Secrets, Fasting Girls, Hunger Hurts but Starving Works* and *Dying to be Thin* help to normalize anorexia in readers' minds. One site explains that their: "website is to help those who are wanting to become anorexic, and for those who are feeling weak," where weak means eating.

[W]ith the proliferation of porn and file sharing sites, democracy and free speech have had their limits tested.

Pro-ana sites often try to support their arguments by posting articles like "UW Study: Eat Less, Live Longer!" and "Fewer calories = Longer Life!," which support eating less, but are taken out of context and extrapolated to the extreme. But the real power of these sites comes from the reinforcing and normalizing of the belief among members that anorexia sufferers have merely chosen to live a certain way, much as someone would choose a style of clothing. Usually pro-ana sites don't actively recruit members, although you could say that they definitely encourage it, and many members already have a history of anorexia. Pro-ana sites were at their height during the period 2000–2003, but since then there has been a dramatic drop off rate, put down to heavy Internet censorship of the sites.

Treating Only Symptoms

Having the pro-ana (there are also offshoots like pro-bella and pro-mia for bulimia) philosophy explained to you is both surprising and shocking, and one's first reaction is to side with those who want to ban outright all online traces of the movement. After some contemplation, however, you remind yourself that these girls are the sufferers of a very dangerous and misunderstood disorder, and that the pro-ana sites are likely just another manifestation of anorexia. Sure, you could treat this symptom—as I'm sure advocates of censorship believe they are doing—but this ignores the fact that the pro-ana blogs and websites are also a valuable source of information about the lives and psychological make-up of those who have the disorder.

Treatment and prevention of anorexia has always been a daunting task for health professionals. Some health workers explain that it is easier to get young females off hard-drugs than it is for them to treat anorexia, and a recent Penn State University study claimed that: "The mortality rate associated with anorexia is 12 times higher than the death rate of other causes of death for females 15–24 years old."

Treatment and prevention of anorexia has always been a daunting task for health professionals.

The fact that anorexia is such an unforgiving and dangerous disorder is why pro-ana sites are so important, as they can act as a window into what may have started the disorder in the first place, and what it is that keeps the disorder ticking along. And even if you don't consider that there is any medical merit in keeping these sites open, wouldn't it be better to know what young anorexics are thinking and feeling than not? Critics of this approach may argue that this is a mercenary way of getting to grips with a dangerous syndrome like anorexia, and that the censorship of such sites is the only option available. But censorship on the Internet is a tricky business and pro-ana sites are still easily found.

Going Underground

In fact, the pro-ana sites, and their self-harm counterparts, have merely slipped out of mainstream view and gone underground; a scenario that has for a long time been associated with censorship. Hosts of pro-ana sites have become experts at hiding the intentions behind their site, often posting disclaimers on their entry pages that their site is for the support of people with anorexia. Well, I guess they're not lying, as they do support individuals who are anorexic, it's just that the support offered is how anorexics can *maintain* the disorder. Lifestyle, remember? One site has a whole page devoted to telling other pro-ana advocates: "How to stop getting your ana site deleted." Tips include not listing your site with high profile search engines like Google, saving work in case of deletion, and: "Always put up a disclaimer note on your main page telling visitors why it was created. This is so they don't think you're making the page to *ahem* 'turn teenage girls into anorexics.'" Stealth like this is alarming, and more worryingly, it makes it very difficult to sort the harmful websites from those offering genuine support.

The ability to communicate globally is one of the most powerful tools that humans have at their disposal. The Internet is a facilitator of this ability and can therefore aid in fostering community care and responsibility through complex social networks. However, it seems evident that we are still at a critical juncture of our online evolution, as there is still much about our own humanity that shocks, frightens and offends sensibilities.

Censorship Is Harmful

When anorexic young females began writing about their lives in blogs and forums a whole new line of communication instantly opened up, and with that came new hope for parents, health professionals and close friends who have been trying to understand the disorder and the young women for years. But instead of embracing this open dialogue, society displayed moral outrage and sought fit to respond by shutting down the sites, and along with it an invaluable source of insight into a vexing and deadly disorder. Worse still, censorship has led to pro-ana sites employing new tactics to avoid detection and deletion; often, of all things, portraying themselves as anorexia *help* sites; an arguably much more dangerous framing.

Hosts of pro-ana sites have become experts at hiding the intentions behind their site, often posting disclaimers on their entry pages that their site is for the support of people with anorexia.

It's deeply regrettable that censorship has achieved nothing more than burying the problem away from mainstream view. Hidden away, pro-ana sites continue to flourish away from the prying eyes of those who can and wish to help. Shame on us, if out-of-sight out-of-mind is the best that we can do for those suffering this insidious disorder.

Organizations to Contact

The editors have compiled the following list of organizations concerned with the issues debated in this book. The descriptions are derived from materials provided by the organizations. All have publications or information available for interested readers. The list was compiled on the date of publication of the present volume; names, addresses, phone and fax numbers, and e-mail and Internet addresses may change. Be aware that many organizations take several weeks or longer to respond to inquiries, so allow as much time as possible.

Beatbullying

Rochester House, London   SE19 2AT
  United Kingdom
+44 20 8771 3377 • fax: +44 20 8771 8550
e-mail: info@beatbullying.org
Web site: www.beatbullying.org

Beatbullying works with children and teenagers across the UK to provide important opportunities to change their lives and outlook positively. In particular, the organization works with those so deeply affected by bullying that they fear going to school. Beatbullying also seeks to effect change in bullies' behavior, working with them to take responsibility and a sense of ownership over their actions. Videos, news, and lesson plans, such as the Friendship and Peer Pressure Lesson Plan, are available online.

Childnet International

Studio 14 Brockley Cross Business Centre, London   SE4 2PD
  United Kingdom
+44 20 7639 6967 • fax: +44 20 7639 7027
e-mail: info@childnet.com
Web site: www.childnet.com

The Childnet International Web site gives Internet safety advice and links for children, teenagers, parents, and teachers. The organization is dedicated to helping young people use the Net constructively, showcasing quality content, and enabling others to use available resources and develop new projects. Policy papers and annual reviews are available online.

ConnectSafely
Web site: www.connectsafely.org

ConnectSafely is a forum for parents, teens, educators, and advocates designed to give teens and parents a voice in the public discussion about youth online safety. The site offers tips, as well as other resources, for safe social networking. It also includes current articles on issues related to social networking sites.

Cyberbully411
Web site: www.cyberbully411.org

Cyberbully411 provides resources and opportunities for discussion and sharing for teenagers who want to know more about—or have been victims of—online harassment. The Web site, created by the nonprofit Internet Solutions for Kids, Inc., invites teenagers to share their stories and download tips and information on cyberbullying, depression, and other relevant topics.

Federal Trade Commission (FTC)
600 Pennsylvania Avenue NW, Washington, DC 20580
(202) 326-2222
Web site: www.ftc.gov

The Federal Trade Commission (FTC) deals with issues of the everyday economic life. It is the only federal agency with both consumer protection and competition jurisdiction. The FTC strives to enforce laws and regulations and to advance consumers' interests by sharing its expertise with federal and state legislatures and U.S. and international government agencies. Publications such as "Social Networking Sites: A Parent's Guide" can be downloaded from its Web site.

Bibliography

Books

Jason Alba

I'm on LinkedIn—Now What???: A Guide to Getting the Most Out of LinkedIn. 2nd ed. Cupertino, CA: Happy About, 2009.

Julia Angwin

Stealing MySpace: The Battle to Control the Most Popular Website in America. New York: Random House, 2009.

Patti Anklam

Net Work: A Practical Guide to Creating and Sustaining Networks at Work and in the World. Boston: Elsevier/Butterworth-Heinemann, 2007.

Dave Awl

Facebook Me! A Guide to Having Fun with Your Friends and Promoting Your Projects on Facebook. Berkeley, CA: Peachpit Press, 2009.

Jack Balkin et al., eds.

Cybercrime: Digital Cops in a Networked Environment. New York: New York University Press, 2007.

John Bush, ed.

Child Safety: From Sexual Predators. CreateSpace, 2008.

Christina Garsten and Helena Wulff

New Technologies at Work: People, Screens, and Social Virtuality. Oxford, UK: Berg, 2003.

Jay Goldman   *Facebook Cookbook: Building
                       Applications to Grow Your Facebook
                       Empire.* Sebastopol, CA: O'Reilly
                       Media, 2009.

Steve Holzner   *Facebook Marketing: Leverage Social
                       Media to Grow Your Business.*
                       Indianapolis, IN: Que Publishing,
                       2009.

Dennis Howitt   *Sex Offenders and the Internet.*
and Kerry   Hoboken, NJ: John Wiley & Sons,
Sheldon   2007.

John Maver and   *Essential Facebook Development: Build
Cappy Popp   Successful Applications for the
                       Facebook Platform.* Upper Saddle
                       River, NJ: Addison-Wesley
                       Professional, 2010.

Samuel McQuade   *Cyber Bullying: Protecting Kids and
III, James Colt,   Adults from Online Bullies.* Westport,
and Nancy Meyer   CT: Praeger, 2009.

Ben Mezrich   *The Accidental Billionaires: The
                       Founding of Facebook: A Tale of Sex,
                       Money, Genius and Betrayal.* New
                       York: Doubleday, 2009.

Mike O'Neil and   *Rock the World with Your Online
Lori Ruff   Presence: Your Ticket to a
                       Multi-Platinum LinkedIn Profile.*
                       Chicago: Networlding, 2010.

John Pospisil   *Hacking MySpace: Customizations and
                       Mods to Make MySpace Your Space.*
                       Indianapolis, IN: Wiley, 2006.

Mike Ribble and Gerald Bailey	*Digital Citizenship in Schools.* Eugene, OR: International Society for Technology in Education, 2007.
Jean Marie Rusin	*Poison Pen Pal: Secrets, Lies, and Online Predators.* Bloomington, IN: AuthorHouse, 2006.
Diana Saco	*Cybering Democracy: Public Space and the Internet.* Minneapolis: University of Minnesota Press, 2002.
Neal Schaffer	*Windmill Networking: Understanding, Leveraging & Maximizing LinkedIn; An Unofficial, Step-by-Step Guide to Creating & Implementing Your LinkedIn Brand.* Charleston, SC: BookSurge Publishing, 2009.
Clara Chung-wai Shih	*The Facebook Era: Tapping Online Social Networks to Build Better Products, Reach New Audiences, and Sell More Stuff.* Boston: Prentice Hall, 2009.
Mike Sullivan	*Online Predators: A Parent's Guide for the Virtual Playground.* Longwood, FL: Xulon Books, 2008.
Emily Vander Veer	*Facebook: The Missing Manual.* 2nd ed. Sebastopol, CA: O'Reilly, 2010.

Periodicals

Bruce Bower	"Growing Up Online: Young People Jump Headfirst into the Internet's World," *Science News*, June 17, 2006.

Bruce Bower   "Internet Seduction: Online Sex
                       Offenders Prey on At-Risk Teens,"
                       Science News, February 23, 2008.

Curriculum   "Teens Share Sexually Explicit
Review   Messages: Simple Rebellion or
                       Dangerous Behavior?" May 2009.

Economist   "Primates on Facebook: Even Online,
                       the Neocortex Is the Limit," February
                       26, 2009.

Martin Fackler   "In Korea, a Boot Camp Cure for
                       Web Obsession," *New York Times*,
                       November 18, 2007.

Florida Parishes   "Loranger Teen Booked in Threats to
Bureau   Harm Other Teen, Cyberstalking,"
                       The Advocate, July 12, 2007.

Adam Geller   "VA Gunman Had 2 Past Stalking
                       Cases," Associated Press, April 18,
                       2007.

Lev Grossman   "The Hyperconnected," *Time*, April 5,
                       2007.

Ann Doss Helms   "5 Teachers Disciplined for Facebook
                       Postings," *Charlotte Observer*,
                       November 12, 2008.

Arik Hesseldahl   "Social Networking Sites a 'Hotbed'
                       for Spyware," *BusinessWeek*, August
                       18, 2006.

Yvonne Jewkes   "Policing the Filth: The Problems of
and Carol   Investigating Online Child
Andrews   Pornography in England and Wales,"
                       Policing and Society, March 2005.

Monica Jones   "Your Child and the Internet: Tips to
                        Keep Them Safe on the Information
                        Superhighway," *Ebony*, March 2006.

Rick Kirschner   "Why the Need for Human
                        Connection?" *Persuasive
                        Communication and Life Skills*, July
                        29, 2008.

Karen Klein   "How to Start a Social Networking
                        Site," *Los Angeles Times*, June 9, 2009.

Maureen   "Misbehavior in Cyberspace: The
Macfarlane   Rise in Social Networking Sites and
                        Chat Rooms Intermingles Free
                        Expression and Student Safety in
                        Cyberspace," *School Administrator*,
                        October 2007.

Claire Cain Miller   "Venture Capitalists Look for a
                        Return to the A B C's," *New York
                        Times*, July 6, 2009.

Justin Pope   "Colleges Warn About Networking
                        Sites," Associated Press, August 2,
                        2006.

Benjamin Radford   "Predator Panic: A Closer Look,"
                        Skeptical Inquirer, September 2006.

James Randerson   "Social Networking Sites Don't
                        Deepen Friendships," *Guardian*,
                        September 10, 2007.

Paul M.   "Virtual Child Porn's Very Real
Rodriguez   Consequences," *Insight on the News*,
                        May 27, 2002.

Christine Rosen	"Virtual Friendship and the New Narcissism," *New Atlantis*, Summer 2007.
Brad Stone	"Social Networking's Next Phase," *New York Times*, March 3, 2007.
Jon Swarz	"Social Networking Sites Boost Productivity," *USA Today*, October 8, 2008.
Clive Thompson	"Brave New World of Digital Intimacy," *New York Times*, September 7, 2008.
James Tozer	"Husband Dumps His Wife with Online Message in 'World's First Divorce by Facebook.'" *Daily Mail* (UK), February 9, 2009.
Sarah Jane Tribble	"The Social Network as a Career Safety Net," *New York Times*, August 13, 2008.

Internet Sources

Denise Caruso	"Why Is Facebook So Addictive?" *Salon*, August 7, 2008. www.salon.com.
Center for the Digital Future	"Annual Internet Survey by the Center for the Digital Future Finds Shifting Trends Among Adults About the Benefits and Consequences of Children Going Online," Center for the Digital Future at USC Annenberg School for Communication, 2008. www.digitalcenter.org.